FOOD LOVERS

CUPCAKES AND BAKES

RECIPES SELECTED BY JONNIE LÉGER

Trans
Atlantic
Press

For best results when cooking the recipes in this book, buy fresh ingredients and follow the instructions carefully. Note that as a general rule vulnerable groups such as the very young, elderly people, pregnant women, convalescents and anyone suffering from an illness should avoid dishes that contain raw or lightly cooked eggs.

For all recipes, quantities are given in standard U.S. cups and imperial measures, followed by the metric equivalent. Follow one set or the other, but not a mixture of both because conversions may not be exact. Standard spoon and cup measurements are level and are based on the following:

1 tsp = 5 ml, 1 tbsp = 15 ml, 1 cup = 250 ml / 8 fl oz.

Note that Australian standard tablespoons are 20 ml, so Australian readers should use 3 tsp in place of 1 tbsp when measuring small quantities.

The electric oven temperatures in this book are given for conventional ovens with top and bottom heat. When using a fan oven, the temperature should be decreased by about 20–40°F / 10–20°C – check the oven manufacturer's instruction book for further guidance. The cooking times given should be used as an approximate guideline only.

CONTENTS

TOFFEE CUPCAKES

Ingredients

2¼ cups / 225 g all-purpose (plain) flour

Scant ½ cup / 90 g superfine (caster) sugar

2 tsp baking powder

Pinch of salt

1 egg, beaten

²/3 cup / 150 ml milk

¼ cup / 50 ml sunflower oil

1 tsp vanilla extract

For the toffee cream:

Heaped ½ cup / 115 g sugar

2 tbsp water

Pinch of salt

1¾ cups / 400 ml whipping cream

For the caramel sauce:

1¼ cups / 250 g superfine (caster) sugar

4 tbsp water

²/3 cup / 150 ml whipping cream

4 tbsp / 50 g butter

Method

Prep and cook time: 40 min plus 40 min chilling time

1 Preheat the oven to 400°F (200°C / Gas Mark 6). Line a 12-hole muffin pan with paper muffin cases.

2 Sift the flour, sugar, baking powder and salt into a large bowl.

3 Put the egg, milk, oil and vanilla extract in a jug and whisk together with a fork. Stir into the dry ingredients until combined. Spoon the mixture equally into the muffin cases.

4 Bake in the oven for about 20 minutes until golden brown and risen. Leave in the pan for 5 minutes and then transfer to a wire rack and leave to cool.

5 Meanwhile, make the toffee cream. Put the sugar, water and salt in a saucepan and cook over a medium heat, stirring once, until sugar has dissolved. Continue cooking, but do not stir, until sugar turns golden amber. Remove from the heat.

6 Slowly pour the cream into the pan, taking care as it will spatter. Heat gently, stirring until combined. Pour the caramel cream into a large bowl and leave to cool. Chill in the refrigerator for about 40 minutes until cold, stirring occasionally.

7 To make the caramel sauce, put the sugar into a heavy-based skillet (frying pan) and stir in the water. Heat gently, tilting the pan, until the sugar has dissolved. Do not stir or the sugar will crystallize. Increase the heat and bubble for 4–5 minutes until golden brown. Remove from the heat and carefully stir in the cream and butter. Pour into a jug or bowl and leave to cool.

8 To serve, whisk the toffee cream until soft peaks form. Spoon into a piping bag and pipe on top of the cold cupcakes. Drizzle with caramel sauce and serve immediately.

Makes 12

ORANGE MUFFINS

Ingredients

For the muffins:

5 tbsp / 75 g butter, melted

1 egg, lightly beaten

¾ cup / 175 ml plain yogurt

Juice and finely grated zest of
1 large orange

Juice ½ lemon

2½ cups / 250 g all-purpose
(plain) flour

1 tbsp baking powder

¾ cup / 150 g sugar

1 tbsp orange marmalade

For the glaze:

Juice and finely grated zest of
1 large orange

6 tbsp confectioners' (icing) sugar

2 tsp orange marmalade

Method

Prep and cook time: 40 min

1 Heat the oven to 375ºF (180ºC / Gas Mark 5). Arrange paper baking cups in a 10-hole muffin pan.

2. Combine the butter, egg, yogurt, orange juice and zest and lemon juice in a mixing bowl. Stir in the flour, baking powder and sugar. Gently stir in the marmalade.

3 Spoon the mixture into the paper cases, almost to the top. Bake for 25 minutes until golden and risen. Leave to stand for 5 minutes, then place on a wire rack to cool.

4 For the glaze, beat all the ingredients together in a bowl. The mixture should be thick enough to coat the back of a spoon, but still fluid.

5 Spoon the glaze over the muffins.

Makes 10

CHOCOLATE APPLE MUFFINS

Ingredients

2¾ cups / 275 g all-purpose (plain) flour

4 tbsp cocoa powder

Heaped 1 cup / 225 g light brown sugar

1 tbsp baking powder

¼ cup / 50 ml sunflower oil

4 tbsp / 50 g butter, melted

2 eggs

¾ cup / 175 ml milk

1 cooking apple, peeled, cored and diced

For the decoration:

2½ oz / 75 g white chocolate (20% cocoa butter), coarsely grated

Method

Prep and cook time: 35 min

1 Heat the oven to 350ºF (180ºC / Gas Mark 4). Grease 12 muffin tins.

2 Sift the flour, cocoa, sugar and baking powder into a mixing bowl.

3 Beat the oil and butter with the eggs and milk until combined. Stir lightly into the dry ingredients but don't over-mix; the mixture should be slightly lumpy. Fold in the apples.

4 Spoon into the muffin tins until three-quarters full.

5 Bake for 20–25 minutes until risen and golden and a skewer inserted into the middle comes out clean. Cool in the tins for 5 minutes then place on a wire rack to cool.

6 Scatter the grated white chocolate over the top of the muffins.

Makes 12

ICED CUPCAKES

Ingredients

1 stick / 115 g butter

½–⅔ cup / 120 g superfine (caster) sugar

2 eggs, beaten

Heaped 1 cup / 120 g self-rising flour

½ tsp baking powder

1 tsp vanilla extract

For the frosting:

1¼ cup / 170 g confectioners' (icing) sugar

2 tbsp lemon juice

1 tsp hot water

Few drops pink food coloring

Pink and white sprinkles, to decorate

Method

Prep and cook time: 30 min

1 Preheat the oven to 350°F (180°C / Gas Mark 4). Line a 12-hole muffin pan with paper cases.

2 Put the butter and sugar in a large bowl and, using an electric whisk, beat together until light and fluffy.

3 Add the eggs gradually, beating well after each addition. Sift in the flour and baking powder and gently fold into the mixture. Stir in the vanilla extract. Spoon the mixture equally into the paper cases.

4 Bake in the oven for 12–15 minutes until springy to the touch. Transfer to a wire rack and leave to cool.

5 When cold, make the frosting. Sift the confectioners' (icing) sugar into a large bowl and gradually stir in the lemon juice and water until smooth.

6 Put half the frosting in another bowl and add a few drops of pink food coloring.

7 Spoon a little frosting on each cupcake and smooth the surface with a palette knife. Decorate with pink and white sprinkles and leave to set.

Makes 12

ESPRESSO CUPCAKES WITH MASCARPONE CREAM

Ingredients

5 tbsp / 75 g butter

2½ cups / 250 g all-purpose (plain) flour

2 tsp baking powder

¼ cup / 50 g light brown sugar

1 egg, beaten

7 tbsp cold strong black coffee

3 tbsp buttermilk

For the mascarpone cream:

1½ sticks / 175 g butter, softened

2¾ cups / 350 g confectioners' (icing) sugar

1 cup / 225 g mascarpone

2 tsp cold strong black coffee

Ground cinnamon for dusting

Method

Prep and cook time: 40 min

1 Preheat the oven to 350°F (180°C / Gas Mark 4). Line a 12-hole muffin pan with paper cases.

2 Melt the butter. Sift the flour and baking powder into a large bowl. Stir in the sugar.

3 Stir the egg and melted butter together and then stir in the coffee and buttermilk. Gently stir into the dry ingredients until just combined. Spoon the mixture equally into the paper cases.

4 Bake in the oven for about 25 minutes until risen and springy to the touch. Leave in the pan for 5 minutes and then place on a wire rack to cool.

5 To make the mascarpone cream, beat the butter in a large bowl until soft and then sift in the sugar. Gradually add the mascarpone until smooth and creamy. Stir in the coffee.

6 Spoon a little mascarpone cream on top of each cupcake and sprinkle with ground cinnamon to decorate before serving.

Makes 12

VANILLA CUPCAKES WITH BUTTERCREAM FROSTING

Ingredients

1½ sticks / 175 g butter

¾–1 cup / 175 g sugar

1 tsp vanilla extract

4 eggs, beaten

1½ cups / 175 g self-rising flour

For the buttercream:

5 tbsp / 75 g butter

1⅓ cups / 175 g confectioners'
(icing) sugar

Few drops vanilla extract

To decorate:

12 raspberries

Method

Prep and cook time: 35 min

1 Heat the oven to 350°F (180°C / Gas Mark 4).
Place paper cases in a 12-hole bun tin.

2 Cream the butter and sugar in a mixing bowl
until light and fluffy.

3 Stir in the vanilla. Gradually beat in the
eggs, beating well.

4 Sift in the flour and gently fold into the
mixture until combined.

5 Spoon into the paper cases and bake for
20 minutes until golden and risen.

6 Leave in the tins for 5 minutes. Place on a
wire rack to cool.

7 For the buttercream, beat the butter in a
bowl until soft.

8 Sift in the confectioners' sugar and beat
well. Stir in the vanilla.

9 Spoon into a piping bag. Pipe a whirl onto
each cake. Top with a raspberry.

Makes 12

CHOCOLATE CHERRY CAKES

Ingredients

3 oz / 75 g milk chocolate (25% cocoa solids), chopped

1 stick / 115 g butter

1 cup / 200 g superfine (caster) sugar

1 egg, beaten

1 cup / 250 ml buttermilk

1 tsp vanilla extract

2½ heaped cups / 275 g all-purpose (plain) flour

1 tsp baking soda (bicarbonate of soda)

12 fresh cherries with stems

Method

Prep and cook time: 35 min

1 Preheat the oven to 375°F (190°C / Gas Mark 5). Line a 12-hole muffin pan with paper muffin cases.

2 Break the chocolate into a heatproof bowl and add the butter. Microwave on High for 1 minute or until softened. Stir and microwave for a further 15 seconds until melted. Alternatively, melt in a bowl standing over a saucepan of gently simmering water. Remove from the heat and stir until smooth. Leave to cool slightly.

3 Put the sugar, egg, buttermilk and vanilla extract in a large bowl and mix together. Stir in the melted chocolate.

4 Sift in the flour and baking soda (bicarbonate of soda) and gently stir into the mixture until combined.

5 Spoon the mixture equally into the muffin cases. Place a cherry into the center of each cake.

6 Bake in the oven for about 25 minutes until the cakes are springy to the touch. Leave in the pan for 5 minutes and then transfer to a wire rack and leave to cool.

Makes 12

CUPCAKES WITH ICE CREAM LAYERS

Ingredients

1 stick / 120 g butter

½ cup / 110 g superfine (caster) sugar

1 tsp vanilla extract

Heaped 1 cup / 120 g self-rising flour

Pinch of salt

1 tsp cornstarch (cornflour)

2 eggs, beaten

For the ice cream filling:

12 scoops strawberry ice cream

For the chocolate topping:

4 tbsp / 50 g butter

¼ cup / 20 g cocoa powder

½ cup / 75 g confectioners' (icing) sugar

1 tsp vanilla extract

Method

Prep and cook time: 40 min

1 Heat the oven to 350°F (180°C / Gas Mark 4). Place paper cases in a 12-hole bun tin.

2 Cream the butter and sugar until light and fluffy. Stir in the vanilla.

3 Sift in the flour, salt and cornstarch (cornflour) and lightly fold into the mixture alternately with the eggs until well blended.

4 Spoon into the paper cases and bake for about 20–25 minutes until golden brown and springy to the touch.

5 Allow to stand for 5 minutes, and then place on a wire rack to cool.

6 Split each cupcake into three, using a sharp knife. Place half a scoop of strawberry ice cream on one layer and spread quickly over the cake. Top with a layer of cupcake. Spread with another half scoop of strawberry ice cream and top with the third layer of cake. Place the cakes in the freezer.

7 For the chocolate topping, beat the butter until soft and sift the cocoa powder over. Stir well, then sift the confectioners' (icing) sugar over and add the vanilla. Mix well.

8 Spread the topping over the top of each cake. Place the cakes back in the freezer until you are ready to serve.

Makes 12

CHOCOLATE MUFFINS WITH CREAM FILLING

Ingredients

6 oz / 175 g bittersweet (plain) chocolate (70% cocoa solids), chopped

4 tbsp / 50 g butter

3 heaped cups / 375 g self-rising flour

1 tbsp baking powder

4 tbsp cocoa powder

½ cup / 100 g superfine (caster) sugar

1 egg

Scant 1½ cups / 350 ml milk

¾ cup / 75 g hazelnuts

1¼ cups / 300 ml whipping cream

Confectioners' (icing) sugar for dusting

Method

Prep and cook time: 45 min

1 Preheat the oven to 400°F (200°C / Gas Mark 6). Grease a 12-hole muffin pan.

2 Break the chocolate into a heatproof bowl and add the butter. Melt the chocolate and butter in a bowl standing over a saucepan of gently simmering water. Remove from the heat and stir once. Leave to cool slightly.

3 Sift the flour, baking powder and cocoa powder into a large bowl. Stir in the sugar.

4 Mix the egg and milk together and slowly stir into the melted chocolate. Stir the mixture into the dry ingredients until only just combined.

5 Spoon the mixture equally into the muffin cups and scatter a few hazelnuts over the top of each muffin.

6 Bake in the oven for 20–25 minutes until well risen and firm to the touch. Leave in the pan for 5 minutes and then place on a wire rack to cool.

7 Whisk the cream until stiff but not dry and spoon into a piping bag. When the muffins are cold, split them in half.

8 Pipe a swirl of cream on the bottom half of each muffin. Replace the tops and dust lightly with sifted confectioners' (icing) sugar.

Makes 12

REDCURRANT AND BLUEBERRY MUFFINS

Ingredients

2 eggs

4 tbsp / 50 g butter, melted

¾ cup / 175 ml milk

1 tsp vanilla extract

1¾ cups / 175 g all-purpose (plain) flour

¼ cup / 50 g sugar

2 tsp baking powder

1½ cups / 175 g mixed redcurrants and blueberries

For the topping:

1 cup / 120 g confectioners' (icing) sugar

1 tbsp hot water

Few drops of pink coloring

Method

Prep and cook time: 35 min

1 Heat the oven to 400°F (200°C / Gas Mark 6). Place paper cases in a 12-hole muffin pan.

2 Mix together the eggs, butter, milk and vanilla.

3 Sift the flour, sugar and baking powder into a mixing bowl and add the egg mixture. Stir gently with a fork until just combined. Fold in the redcurrants and blueberries.

4 Spoon into the paper cases and bake for 20–25 minutes until well risen and firm.

5 Leave to stand for 5 minutes then place on a wire rack to cool.

6 For the topping, sift the confectioners' (icing) sugar into a bowl and gradually beat in the hot water and a few drops of coloring. Drizzle over the cold muffins and leave to set.

Makes 12

APRICOT AND GINGER MUFFINS

Ingredients

4 tbsp / 50 g butter, plus extra to grease the pan

1½ cups / 150 g all-purpose (plain) flour

½ tbsp baking powder

Pinch of salt

1 egg

¼ cup / 50 g superfine (caster) sugar

7 tbsp / 100 ml milk

1 tsp vanilla extract

¾ cup / 115 g chopped fresh apricots

For the topping:

5 tbsp / 75 g butter

2 tbsp corn (golden) syrup

1 cup / 125 g confectioners' (icing) sugar

½ cup / 75 g chopped candied (crystallized) ginger

Method

Prep and cook time: 45 min

1 Preheat the oven to 400°F (200°C / Gas Mark 6). Grease a 6-hole muffin pan.

2 Melt the butter. Sift the flour, baking powder and salt into a large bowl.

3 Mix together the egg, sugar, milk, vanilla extract and melted butter. Stir into the dry ingredients quickly until only just combined and still slightly lumpy.

4 Gently fold in the apricots. Spoon the mixture equally into the muffin cups.

5 Bake in the oven for 25–30 minutes until risen and golden brown.

6 Meanwhile, make the topping. Heat the butter, corn (golden) syrup and confectioners' (icing) sugar in a small saucepan over a medium heat for about 5 minutes until smooth. Stir in the ginger pieces.

7 Spoon on top of the partially cooked muffins for the last 5–8 minutes of the cooking time.

8 When the muffins are cooked and the topping is crisp, leave in the pan for 5 minutes and then transfer to a wire rack and leave to cool.

Makes 6

CHRISTMAS CUPCAKES

Ingredients

3 tsp / 20 g butter

2 eggs

½–⅔ cup / 120 g superfine (caster) sugar

3 tbsp whipping cream

½ cup / 115 g mincemeat

1 cup / 120 g self-rising flour

½ tsp baking powder

1 tsp ground cinnamon

½ tsp freshly grated nutmeg

2 tsp sherry

For the decoration:

4 oz / 120 g white marzipan

Red and green food colorings

Confectioners' (icing) sugar for dusting

Method

Prep and cook time: 35 min

1 Preheat the oven to 350°F (180°C / Gas Mark 4). Line a 12-hole muffin pan with paper cases.

2 Melt the butter. Mix the eggs and sugar together and beat in the cream. Gently stir in the mincemeat.

3 Sift in the flour, baking powder, cinnamon and nutmeg and fold in until incorporated.

4 Stir in the sherry and melted butter until well mixed. Spoon the mixture equally into the paper cases.

5 Bake in the oven for 12–15 minutes until risen and springy to the touch. Transfer to a wire rack and leave to cool.

6 Divide the marzipan in half. Knead a few drops of red coloring into one half and of green into the other half.

7 Roll out the marzipan on a surface lightly dusted with confectioners' (icing) sugar. Cut out festive shapes, such as stars and bells, with small cookie cutters.

8 Place the marzipan decorations on top of each cupcake and sift over a thick layer of confectioners' (icing) sugar to decorate.

Makes 12

BUTTERFLY BUNS

Ingredients

2 eggs

1 cup / 110 g self-rising flour

½ teaspoon baking powder

1 stick / 110 g soft butter

½ cup / 110 g sugar

To decorate:

¾ cup / 175 g whipping cream

Confectioners' (icing) sugar

Method

Prep and cook time: 40 min

1 Heat the oven to 325ºF (170ºC / Gas Mark 3). Line a 12-hole muffin pan with paper cases.

2 Put all the ingredients for the cakes into a mixing bowl and whisk with an electric whisk until well combined. Alternatively, beat well with a wooden spoon.

3 Spoon the mixture into the paper cases and bake for about 30 minutes until the cakes are golden and springy to the touch.

4 Carefully cut round the tops of the cake with a cutter or sharp knife and remove the top of each cake. Slice the tops in half to form two 'wings'.

5 Whisk the cream until thick but not stiff. Spoon into a piping bag. Pipe a whirl onto each cake and press the 'wings' into the cream. Sift over a little confectioners' (icing) sugar.

Makes 12

APPLE CAKES

Ingredients

2 eggs

½ cup / 110 g superfine (caster) sugar

1 cup / 110 g self-rising flour

1 stick / 110 g butter, melted

1 apple, peeled and diced

Confectioners' (icing) sugar,
to decorate

Method

Prep and cook time: 25 min

1 Heat the oven to 350ºF (180ºC / Gas 4). Grease a 12-hole bun tin.

2 Whisk the eggs and sugar together in a bowl until light and fluffy.

3 Gently fold in the flour and butter, followed by the apple.

4 Pour the mixture into the bun tin and bake for 8–10 minutes, until golden brown and a skewer inserted into one of the cakes comes out clean. Leave in the tins for 10 minutes, and then place on a wire rack to cool.

5 Sift over a little confectioners' (icing) sugar just before serving.

Makes 12

MINI CHERRY MUFFINS

Ingredients

5 tbsp / 75 g butter

$1/3$ cup / 75 g superfine (caster) sugar

2 eggs, beaten

¾ cup / 75 g self-rising flour

½ tsp almond extract

¾ cup / 110 g candied (glacé) cherries, chopped

For the frosting:

½ cup / 75 g confectioners' (icing) sugar

2 tsp hot water

To decorate:

24 whole fresh cherries

Method

Prep and cook time: 45 min

1 Heat the oven to 350ºF (180ºC / Gas Mark 4). Place paper cases in a 24-cup mini-muffin tin.

2 Beat the butter and sugar until light and fluffy. Gradually add the eggs, a little at a time, and beat well.

3 Sift in the flour and gently fold into the mixture with the almond extract and the cherries.

4 Spoon into the paper cases and bake for 12–15 minutes until golden and springy to the touch.

5 Place on a wire rack to cool.

6 For the frosting, sift the confectioners' (icing) sugar into a bowl and stir in enough hot water to make a thick frosting (icing).

7 Spread a little frosting on each cake and top with a fresh cherry.

Makes 24

CHOCOLATE MUFFINS WITH ORANGE CREAM

Ingredients

1½ sticks / 175 g butter

2 oz / 50g bittersweet (plain) chocolate (70% cocoa solids), chopped

1 cup / 120 g confectioners' (icing) sugar

¾ cup / 75 g all-purpose (plain) flour

1 tbsp cocoa powder

1 cup / 110 g ground almonds

1 tsp baking powder

Pinch of salt

6 egg whites

1 tsp vanilla extract

For the orange cream:

5 tbsp / 75 g butter

1¼ cups / 150 g confectioners' (icing) sugar

Juice of 1 orange

To decorate:

Grated zest

Method

Prep and cook time: 40 min

1 Heat the oven to 375°F (190°C / Gas Mark 5). Grease a 12-hole muffin pan.

2 Melt the butter and chocolate in a heatproof bowl over a pan of simmering (not boiling) water. Remove from the heat and stir gently to combine.

3 Sift the confectioners' (icing) sugar, flour and cocoa into a mixing bowl and stir in the almonds. Add the baking powder and salt.

4 Beat the egg whites lightly and stir into the dry ingredients with the vanilla.

5 Pour into the muffin pan and bake for about 20 minutes until risen and firm.

6 Leave to stand for 5 minutes, and then place on a wire rack to cool.

7 For the orange cream, whisk all the ingredients together in a small bowl until smooth and creamy.

8 Spoon a little orange cream on top of each muffin and decorate with grated orange zest.

Makes 12

FAIRY CAKES
WITH JAM FILLING

Ingredients

1 stick / 110 g butter

½ cup / 110 g superfine (caster) sugar

2 eggs

1 cup / 110 g self-rising flour

1 teaspoon baking powder

½ cup / 75 g strawberry jelly (jam)

Method

Prep and cook time: 30 min

1 Heat the oven to 350°F (180°C / Gas Mark 4). Line a 12-hole muffin pan with paper cases.

2 Put all the ingredients into a mixing bowl and beat well for 2–3 minutes until the mixture is well blended and smooth.

3 Spoon enough of the mixture into the muffin cases to fill one-third full. Add a good teaspoon of jelly (jam) and cover with cake mixture.

4 Bake for 15–20 minutes until the cakes are risen and golden. Cool the cakes on a wire rack.

Makes 12

CHOCOLATE MUFFINS WITH FONDANT FILLING

Ingredients

2 sticks plus 2 tbsp / 250 g butter

Cocoa powder to dust the pan

7 oz / 200 g bittersweet (plain) chocolate (70% cocoa solids), chopped

4 eggs plus 4 egg yolks

1 cup / 200 g superfine (caster) sugar

2 cups / 200 g all-purpose (plain) flour

To decorate:

Fresh cherries

Method

Prep and cook time: 35 min plus 30 min chilling time

1 Melt 3–4 tbsp (50 g) of the butter and use to grease a 9-hole muffin pan. Dust each muffin cup with cocoa powder to completely coat the butter.

2 Break the chocolate into a heatproof bowl and add the remaining butter. Melt the chocolate and butter in a bowl standing over a saucepan of gently simmering water. Remove from the heat and stir until smooth. Leave to cool slightly.

3 Put the eggs, egg yolks and sugar in a large bowl and whisk together using an electric whisk until thick and pale.

4 Sift the flour into the eggs and then beat together.

5 Gradually beat the melted chocolate into the egg mixture until the mixture is completely combined.

6 Spoon the mixture equally into the muffin cups. Chill in the refrigerator for at least 30 minutes.

7 Preheat the oven to 400°F (200°C / Gas Mark 6). Bake the muffins in the oven for 12–15 minutes until the tops have formed a crust and the muffins are starting to come away from the sides of their molds. Leave in the pan for 2 minutes before removing them gently.

8 Serve warm, decorated with a fresh cherry on top.

Makes 9

BLACKBERRY AND RASPBERRY MUFFINS

Ingredients

1¾ cups / 175 g all-purpose (plain) flour

2 teaspoons baking powder

½ cup / 110 g sugar

1 stick / 110 g butter, melted

1 egg

½ cup / 120 ml milk

½ cup / 110 g blackberries

½ cup / 110 g raspberries

For the topping:

2 oz / 50 g finely chopped almonds

¼ cup / 50 g sugar

3 tbsp flour

3 tbsp / 45 g butter, melted

Method

Prep and cook time: 35 min

1 Heat the oven to 350ºF (180ºC / Gas Mark 4). Grease a 12 cup muffin tin.

2 Sift the flour and baking powder into a mixing bowl and stir in the sugar.

3 Beat the melted butter with the egg and milk and gradually stir into the dry ingredients until just mixed but still slightly lumpy.

4 Gently stir in the blackberries and raspberries.

5 Spoon into the muffin cups, filling almost to the top.

6 For the topping, mix all the ingredients together and spoon a little over the top of each muffin.

7 Bake for about 25 minutes until risen and firm.

8 Leave to stand for 5 minutes, then place on a wire rack to cool.

Makes 12

GINGERBREAD BUNS

Ingredients

1 stick / 115 g butter

2½ cups / 250 g all-purpose (plain) flour

1 heaped cup / 225 g superfine (caster) sugar

2 tsp baking powder

2 tsp ground ginger

½ tsp ground cinnamon

2 eggs

3 tbsp honey

3 tbsp ginger syrup and 2 tbsp chopped preserved ginger

¾ cup / 175 ml hot water

Confectioners' (icing) sugar, to decorate

Method

Prep and cook time: 40 min

1 Preheat the oven to 350°F (180°C / Gas Mark 4). Grease a 12-hole muffin pan.

2 Melt the butter. Sift the flour, sugar, baking powder, ginger and cinnamon into a large bowl.

3 Beat together the eggs, honey, ginger syrup and butter until smooth. Stir into the dry ingredients.

4 Add the water and chopped ginger and stir well until combined. Spoon the mixture equally into the muffin cups.

5 Bake in the oven for 20–25 minutes until golden brown and a skewer inserted into the center comes out clean. Leave in the pan for 10 minutes and then transfer to a wire rack and leave to cool.

6 Sift a little confectioners' (icing) sugar over the buns to decorate just before serving.

Makes 12

CHOCOLATE AND BANANA MUFFINS

Ingredients

1 cup / 120 g self-rising flour

2/3 cup / 120 g sugar

1 tsp baking soda (bicarbonate of soda)

Pinch of salt

1/2 tsp ground cinnamon

3 1/2 oz / 100 g bittersweet (plain) chocolate (70% cocoa solids), chopped

1 egg, beaten

1 stick / 120 g butter, melted

1 tsp vanilla extract

2 very ripe bananas

For the topping:

6 banana slices

Melted butter

Method

Prep and cook time: 45 min

1 Heat the oven to 350ºF (180ºC / Gas 4). Grease a 6-hole muffin tin.

2 Sift the flour, sugar, baking soda (bicarbonate of soda) salt and cinnamon into a mixing bowl. Stir in the chopped chocolate.

3 Make a well in the center and add the beaten egg, warm butter and vanilla.

4 Mash the bananas well and stir into the mixture until just combined, but still slightly lumpy.

5 Spoon the mixture into the holes of the muffin tin and top each with a slice of banana. Brush the banana slices with a little melted butter.

6 Bake for 25–30 minutes until firm and risen. Leave in the tin for 5 minutes, then place on a wire rack to cool.

Makes 6

CARROT MUFFINS WITH WALNUTS

Ingredients

Heaped 1 cup / 225 g sugar

3 eggs

1 cup / 200 ml sunflower oil

2 cups / 225 g whole-wheat (wholemeal) flour

1 tsp ground cinnamon

Pinch of salt

12 oz / 350 g grated carrots

1 cup / 175 g walnuts chopped

For the topping:

1 cup / 225 g cream cheese

2 tbsp light brown sugar

1 tbsp orange juice

Cinnamon

Method

Prep and cook time: 40 min plus 30 min chilling time

1 Heat the oven to 350°F (180°C / Gas Mark 4). Place paper cases in a 10-hole bun tin.

2 Beat together the sugar, eggs and oil until light and frothy.

3 Stir in the flour, cinnamon and salt and beat until combined. Stir in the carrots and walnuts.

4 Spoon into the paper cases and bake for 20–25 minutes until firm and risen. Place on a wire rack to cool.

5 For the topping, beat the ingredients together until smooth. Chill for 30 minutes.

6 Spread the topping over the top of the cakes and dust with a little cinnamon.

Makes 10

Published by Transatlantic Press

First published in 2011

Transatlantic Press
38 Copthorne Road, Croxley Green, Hertfordshire WD3 4AQ

© Transatlantic Press

Images and Recipes by StockFood © The Food Image Agency

Recipes selected by Jonnie Léger, StockFood

A catalogue record for this book is available from the British Library.

ISBN 978-1-908533-48-7

Printed in China